Get Updates and More o

Go to this book's companion page at:

www.nolo.com/back-of-book/DEHB.html

When there's an important change to the law affecting this book, we'll post updates. You'll also find articles and other related materials.

More Resources
from Nolo.com

Legal Forms, Books, & Software
Hundreds of do-it-yourself products—all written in plain English, approved, and updated by our in-house legal editors.

Legal Articles
Get informed with thousands of free articles on everyday legal topics. Our articles are accurate, up to date, and reader friendly.

Find a Lawyer
Want to talk to a lawyer? Use Nolo to find a lawyer who can help you with your case.

NOLO
LAW for ALL

18th Edition

Home Business Tax Deductions

Keep What You Earn

Stephen Fishman, J.D.

EIGHTEENTH EDITION	JANUARY 2022
Editor	AMY LOFTSGORDON
Cover Design	SUSAN PUTNEY
Book Design	SUSAN PUTNEY
Proofreading	MARTHA C. BENCO
Index	SONGBIRD INDEXING SERVICES
Printing	SHERIDAN

ISSN: 1932-2402 (print)

ISSN: 2326-0092 (online)

ISBN: 978-1-4133-2920-9 (pbk)

ISBN: 978-1-4133-2921-6 (ebook)

This book covers only United States law, unless it specifically states otherwise.

Please note

Accurate, plain-English legal information can help you solve many of your own legal problems. But this text is not a substitute for personalized advice from a knowledgeable lawyer. If you want the help of a trained professional—and we'll always point out situations in which we think that's a good idea—consult an attorney licensed to practice in your state.

Acknowledgments

Many thanks to:

Amy Loftsgordon and Diana Fitzpatrick for their superb editing

Susan Putney for her outstanding book design

About the Author

Stephen Fishman has dedicated his career as an attorney and author to writing useful, authoritative, and recognized guides on taxes and business law for small businesses, entrepreneurs, independent contractors, and freelancers. He is the author of over 20 books and hundreds of articles, and has been quoted in the *New York Times*, the *Wall Street Journal*, the *Chicago Tribune*, and many other publications. Among his books are *Deduct It! Lower Your Small Business Taxes*, *Tax Deductions for Professionals*, and *Working for Yourself: Law & Taxes for Independent Contractors, Freelancers & Gig Workers of All Types*.

Table of Contents

Introduction

This book is for you if you're one of the millions of Americans who run a business from home. It shows how home business owners can reduce their taxes by taking advantage of the huge array of tax deductions available to them.

Did you know that, if you have a legitimate home business, you might be able to deduct:

- a portion of your rent or mortgage
- expenses for local and business trips, and
- medical expenses for yourself and your family?

All of these deductions—and many others—can add up to substantial tax savings. The IRS will never complain if you don't take all the deductions available to you. In fact, the majority of home business owners miss out on many deductions every year simply because they aren't aware of them—or because they neglect to keep the records necessary to back them up.

That's where this book comes in. It shows you how you can deduct all or most of your business expenses from your federal taxes. This book is not a tax preparation guide—it does not show you how to fill out your tax forms. (By the time you do your taxes, it might be too late to take deductions you could have taken if you had planned the prior year's business spending wisely and kept proper records.) Instead, this book gives you all the information you need to maximize your deductible expenses—and avoid common deduction mistakes. You can (and should) use this book all year long, so that you're ready to take advantage of every available deduction opportunity come April 15.

Now more than ever, you'll need guidance when it comes to understanding your taxes. In 2017, Congress enacted the most sweeping changes to the tax code in over 30 years when it passed the Tax Cuts and Jobs Act (TCJA), which took effect in 2018. Now, in an effort to stave off economic devastation in the wake of the coronavirus (COVID-19) pandemic, Congress has revised the nation's tax laws yet again, temporarily suspending many of the harshest provisions of the TCJA. We explain these changes including:

- tax treatment of the hugely popular Paycheck Protection Program (PPP) loans
- new rules for deducting net operating losses (see Chapter 1)
- changes to bonus and regular depreciation for improvements to nonresidential real property (see Chapter 5)
- new tax credits for employers who retain their payrolls and provide sick leave and family leave (see Chapter 11)
- new tax credits for self-employed business owners impacted by the coronavirus (COVID-19) pandemic (see Chapter 12)
- temporary rules allowing penalty-free withdrawals from retirement accounts (see Chapter 13)
- rules for deducting business-related meals (see Chapter 14), and
- changes affecting charitable contributions (see Chapter 14).

Even if you work with an accountant or another tax professional, you need to learn about home business tax deductions. No tax professional will ever know as much about your business as you do, and you can't expect a hired professional to search high and low for every deduction you might be able to take, especially during the busy tax preparation season. The information in this book will help you provide your tax professional with better records, ask better questions, and obtain better advice. It will also help you evaluate the advice you get from tax professionals, websites, and other sources, so you can make smart decisions about your taxes.

If you do your taxes yourself (as more and more home businesspeople are doing, especially with the help of tax preparation software), your need for knowledge is even greater. Not even the most sophisticated tax preparation program can decide which tax deductions you should take or tell you whether you've overlooked a valuable deduction. This book can be your guide—providing you with practical advice and information so you can rest assured you are taking full advantage of the many deductions available to home business owners.

Get Updates to This Book on Nolo.com

When important changes to the information in this book happen,
we'll post updates online, on a page dedicated to this book:

www.nolo.com/back-of-book/DEHB.html

Some Tax Basics

Once you start your own business, you can begin taking advantage of the many tax deductions available only to business owners. The tax code is full of deductions for businesses—and you are entitled to take them whether you work from home or from a fancy outside office. Before you can start using these deductions to hang on to more of your hard-earned money, however, you need a basic understanding of how businesses pay taxes and how tax deductions work. This chapter gives you all the information you need to get started.

It covers:
- how tax deductions work
- how businesses are taxed
- what expenses businesses can deduct, and
- how to calculate the value of a tax deduction.

How Tax Deductions Work

A tax deduction (also called a "write-off") is an amount of money you are entitled to subtract from your gross income (all the money you make) to determine your taxable income (the amount on which you must pay tax). The more deductions you have, the lower your taxable income will be and the less tax you will have to pay.

Types of Tax Deductions

The three basic types of tax deductions are personal deductions, investment deductions, and business deductions. This book covers only business deductions—the large array of write-offs available to business owners, including those who work out of their homes.

Personal Deductions

For the most part, your personal, living, and family expenses are not tax deductible. For example, you can't deduct the food that you buy for yourself and your family. There are, however, special categories of personal expenses that may be deducted, subject to strict limitations. These include items such as home mortgage interest, state and local taxes (up to an annual limit), charitable contributions, medical expenses above a threshold amount, and interest on education loans. This book does not cover these personal deductions.

Investment Deductions

Many people try to make money by investing money. For example, they might invest in real estate or play the stock market. These people incur all kinds of expenses, such as fees paid to money managers or financial planners, legal and accounting fees, and interest on money borrowed to buy investment property. In the past, these and other investment expenses (also called "expenses for the production of income") were tax deductible, subject to some important limitations. However, the Tax Cuts and Jobs Act (TCJA) eliminated many of these deductions for 2018 through 2025.

Business Deductions

Home business owners usually have to spend money on their businesses— for example, for equipment, supplies, or business travel. Most business expenses are deductible sooner or later. It makes no difference for tax deduction purposes whether you run your business from home or from an outside office or workplace—either way, you are entitled to deduct your legitimate business expenses. This book is about the many deductions available to people who are in business and who happen to work from home.

You Pay Taxes Only on Your Business Profits

The federal income tax law recognizes that you must spend money to make money. Virtually every home business, however small, incurs some expenses. Even someone with a low-overhead business (such as a freelance writer) must buy paper, computer equipment, and office supplies. Some home businesses incur substantial expenses, even exceeding their income.

You are not legally required to pay tax on every dollar your business takes in (your gross business income). Instead, you owe tax only on the amount left over after your business's deductible expenses are subtracted from your gross income (this remaining amount is called your "net profit"). Although some tax deduction calculations can get a bit complicated, the basic math is simple: The more deductions you take, the lower your net profit will be, and the less tax you will have to pay.

> **EXAMPLE:** Karen, a sole proprietor, earned $50,000 this year from her consulting business, which she operates from her home office. Fortunately, she doesn't have to pay income tax on the entire $50,000—her gross income. Instead, she can deduct various business expenses, including a $5,000 home office deduction (see Chapter 6) and a $5,000 deduction for equipment expenses (see Chapter 5). She deducts these expenses from her $50,000 gross income to arrive at her net profit: $40,000. She pays income tax only on this net profit amount.

Claiming Your Deductions

All tax deductions are a matter of legislative grace, which means that you can take a deduction only if it is specifically allowed by one or more provisions of the tax law. You usually do not have to indicate on your tax return which tax law provision gives you the right to take a particular deduction. If you are audited by the IRS, however, you'll have to provide a legal basis for every deduction you take. If the IRS concludes that your deduction wasn't justified, it will deny the deduction and charge you back taxes, interest, and, in some cases, penalties.

Make Sure You Are in Business

Only businesses can claim business tax deductions. This probably seems like a simple concept, but it can get tricky. Even though you might believe you are running a business, the IRS might beg to differ. If your home business doesn't turn a profit for several years in a row, the IRS might decide that you are engaged in a hobby rather than a business. This might not sound like a big deal, but it could have disastrous tax consequences: As a result of the Tax Cuts and Jobs Act, people engaged in hobbies are not entitled to any tax deductions during 2018 through 2025, while businesses can deduct all kinds of expenses.

Fortunately, careful taxpayers can usually avoid this unhappy outcome. (See Chapter 2 for tips that will help you convince the IRS that you really are running a business.)

How Businesses Are Taxed

If your home business earns money (as you undoubtedly hope it will), you will have to pay taxes on your profits. How you pay those taxes will depend on how you have structured your business. So before getting further into the details of tax deductions, it's important to understand what type of business you have formed (a sole proprietorship, partnership, limited liability company, or corporation), and how you will pay tax on your business's profit.

 RESOURCE
Need help figuring out how to structure your business? Although most home businesses are sole proprietorships, that might not be the best business form for you. If you need to decide how to organize a new business or you want to know whether you should change your current business form, refer to *LLC or Corporation? Choose the Right Form for Your Business*, by Anthony Mancuso (Nolo).

Basic Business Entities

Every business, from a part-time operation you run from home while in your jammies to a Fortune 500 multinational company housed in a gleaming skyscraper, has a legal structure. If you're running a business right now, it has a legal form—even if you never made a conscious decision about how it should be legally organized.

Sole Proprietorship—The Most Popular Home Business Entity

A sole proprietorship is a one-owner business. According to the Small Business Administration, 90% of all home businesses are sole proprietorships. Unlike the other business forms, a sole proprietorship has no legal existence separate from the business owner. It cannot sue or be sued, own property in its own name, or file its own tax returns. The business owner (proprietor) personally owns all of the assets of the business and controls its operations. If you're running a one-person home business and you haven't incorporated or formed a limited liability company, you are a sole proprietor. However, you can't be a sole proprietor if two or more people own your home business, unless you are one of two spouses who jointly own and run their home business together. See Chapter 16 for a detailed discussion about how to legally organize a spouse-and-spouse home business.

Other Business Forms You Can Use

Only about 10% of home businesses adopt a business form other than a sole proprietorship. These other forms include:

- **Partnerships.** A partnership is a form of shared ownership and management of a business. The partners contribute money, property, or services to the partnership; in return, they receive a share of the profits it earns, if any. The partners jointly manage the partnership business. A partnership automatically comes into existence whenever two or more people enter into business together to earn a profit and don't incorporate or form a limited liability company. Thus, if you're running a home business with somebody else, you are in a partnership right now (unless you've formed an LLC or a corporation). Although many partners enter into written partnership agreements, no written agreement is required to form a partnership.

- **Corporations.** Unlike a sole proprietorship or partnership, a corporation cannot simply spring into existence—it can only be created by filing incorporation documents with your state government. A corporation is a legal entity distinct from its owners. It can hold title to property, sue and be sued, have bank accounts, borrow money, hire employees, and perform other business functions. For tax purposes, there are two types of corporations: S corporations (also called "small business corporations") and C corporations (also called "regular corporations"). The most important difference between the two types of corporations is how they are taxed. An S corporation pays no taxes itself—instead, its income or loss is passed on to its owners, who must pay personal income taxes on their share of the corporation's profits. A C corporation is a separate taxpaying entity that pays taxes on its profits (see "Tax Treatment," below).

- **Limited liability companies.** The limited liability company (LLC) is like a sole proprietorship or partnership in that its owners (called members) jointly own and manage the business and share in the profits. However, an LLC is also like a corporation. Because its owners must file papers with the state to create the LLC, it exists as a separate legal entity, and the LLC structure gives owners some protection from liability for business debts.

Tax Treatment

Your business's legal form will determine how it is treated for tax purposes. The two different ways that business entities can be taxed are: The business itself can be taxed as a separate entity, or the business's profits and losses can be passed through to the owners, who include these amounts on their individual tax returns.

Pass-Through Entities: Sole Proprietorships, Partnerships, S Corporations, and LLCs

Sole proprietorships and S corporations are always pass-through entities. LLCs and partnerships are almost always pass-through entities as well— partnerships and multiowner LLCs are automatically taxed as partnerships when they are created. One-owner LLCs are automatically taxed like sole proprietorships. However, LLC and partnership owners have the option of choosing to have their entities taxed as C corporations or S corporations by filing elections with the IRS. This is rarely done.

A pass-through entity does not pay any taxes itself. Instead, the business's profits or losses are passed through to its owners, who include them on their own personal tax returns (IRS Form 1040). If a profit is passed through to the owner, the owner must add that money to any income from other sources and pay tax on the total amount. If a loss is passed through, the owner can generally use it to offset income from other sources—for example, salary from a job, interest, investment income, or a spouse's income (as long as the couple files a joint tax return). The owner can subtract the business loss from this other income, which leaves a lower total subject to tax.

> EXAMPLE: Lisa is a sole proprietor who works part time from home doing engineering consulting. During her first year in business, she incurs $10,000 in expenses and earns $5,000, giving her a $5,000 loss from her business. She reports this loss on IRS Schedule C, which she files with her personal income tax return (Form 1040). Because Lisa is a sole proprietor, she can deduct this $5,000 loss from any income she has, including her $100,000 annual salary from her engineering job. This saves her about $2,000 in total taxes for the year.

Owners of pass-through entities qualify for a new pass-through income tax deduction of up to 20% of their business income under the Tax Cuts and Jobs Act. See Chapter 7 for a detailed discussion.

Although pass-through entities don't pay taxes, their income and expenses must still be reported to the IRS as follows:

- **Sole proprietors** must file IRS Schedule C, *Profit or Loss From Business*, with their tax returns. This form lists all the proprietor's business income and deductible expenses.
- **Partnerships** are required to file an annual tax form (Form 1065, *U.S. Return of Partnership Income*) with the IRS. Form 1065 is used to report partnership revenues, expenses, gains, and losses. The partnership must also provide each partner with an IRS Schedule K-1, *Partner's Share of Income, Deductions, Credits, etc.*, listing the partner's share of partnership income and expenses (copies of these schedules must also be attached to IRS Form 1065). Partners must then file IRS Schedule E, *Supplemental Income and Loss*, with their individual income tax returns, showing their partnership income and deductions.
- **S corporations** must file information returns with the IRS on Form 1120-S, *U.S. Income Tax Return for an S Corporation*, showing how much the business earned or lost and each shareholder's portion of the corporate income or loss. Unlike with the other pass-through entities, S corporation owners ordinarily work as employees

of their corporation. This can help them maximize the new 20% pass-through tax deduction (see Chapter 7 for more information).

- **An LLC** with only one member is treated like a sole proprietorship for tax purposes. The member reports profits, losses, and deductions on Schedule C—just like a sole proprietor. An LLC with two or more members is ordinarily treated like a partnership: The LLC must prepare and file IRS Form 1065, *U.S. Return of Partnership Income*, showing the allocation of profits, losses, credits, and deductions passed through to the members. The LLC must also prepare and distribute to each member a Schedule K-1 showing the member's allocations of profits, losses, credits, and deductions.

Regular C Corporations—Creating Two Taxable Entities

A regular C corporation is the only business form that is not a pass-through entity. Instead, a C corporation is taxed separately from its owners. C corporations must pay income taxes on their net income and file corporate tax returns with the IRS, using Form 1120, *U.S. Corporation Income Tax Return*, or Form 1120-A, *U.S. Corporation Short-Form Income Tax Return*. They also have their own income tax rates. Starting in 2018, the tax rate for regular C corporations was reduced from a top rate of 35% to a flat tax of 21% on all C corporation income. See IRS Publication 542, *Corporations*, for more information.

When you form a C corporation, you have to take charge of two separate taxpayers: your corporation and yourself. Your C corporation must pay tax on all of its income. You pay personal income tax on C corporation income only when it is distributed to you in the form of salary, bonuses, or dividends. However, you might have to pay special penalty taxes if you keep too much money in your corporation to avoid having to pay personal income tax on it.

C corporations can take all the same business tax deductions that pass-through entities take. In addition, because a C corporation is a separate tax-paying entity, it may provide its employees with tax-free fringe benefits, then deduct the entire cost of the benefits from the corporation's income as a business expense. No other form of business entity can do this. (Although they are corporations, S corporations cannot deduct the cost of benefits provided to shareholders who hold more than 2% of the corporate stock.)

What Businesses Can Deduct

Business owners, whether they work at home or elsewhere, can deduct several broad categories of business expenses:

- start-up expenses
- operating expenses
- capital expenses, and
- inventory costs.

A 20% pass-through tax deduction is also available to pass-through business entities (any business entity other than a regular C corporation). This section provides an introduction to each of these deduction categories (they are covered in greater detail in later chapters).

Start-Up Expenses

Start-up expenses are those you incur to get your home business up and running—such as license fees, advertising costs, attorneys' and accounting fees, market research, and office supplies expenses. Start-up costs are not currently deductible—that is, you cannot deduct them all in the year in which you incur them. However, you can deduct up to $5,000 in start-up costs in the first year your new business is in operation. You must deduct amounts over $5,000 over the next 15 years. Most home business owners should be able to avoid incurring substantial start-up expenses. (See Chapter 3 for a detailed discussion of deducting start-up expenses.)

Operating Expenses

Operating expenses are the ongoing day-to-day costs a business incurs to stay in business. They include such things as rent, utilities, salaries, supplies, travel expenses, car expenses, and repairs and maintenance. These expenses (unlike start-up expenses) are currently deductible—that is, you can deduct them all in the year when you pay them. (See Chapter 4 for more on operating expenses.)

Capital Expenses

Capital assets are things you buy for your business that have a useful life of more than one year, such as equipment, vehicles, books, office furniture, machinery, and patents you buy from others. These costs, called capital expenses, are considered to be part of your investment in your business, not day-to-day operating expenses.

The cost of business real estate—buildings and building components— must always be deducted over many years, a process called depreciation. Commercial real estate is depreciated over 39 years. However, the cost of personal property used in business—computers, for example—can usually be deducted in a single year using 100% bonus depreciation (available through 2022) or Section 179 of the tax code. Bonus depreciation and Section 179 are discussed in detail in Chapter 5.

Pass-Through Tax Deduction

Business owners (other than those who have formed a C corporation) may qualify for a special pass-through tax deduction starting in 2018 through 2025. This enables them to deduct from their income taxes up to 20% of their net business income. Certain limitations and requirements must be met to qualify for this 20% pass-through deduction. (See Chapter 7 for more information.)

Inventory

If your home business involves making or buying products, you'll have an inventory. Inventory includes almost anything you make or buy to resell to customers. It doesn't matter whether you manufacture the goods yourself or buy finished goods from someone else and resell them to customers. Inventory doesn't include tools, equipment, or other items that you use in your business; it refers only to items that you buy or make to sell.

Before 2018, you had to deduct inventory costs separately from all other business expenses—you deducted inventory costs as you sold the inventory. However, starting in 2018, smaller businesses have the option to deduct inventory (1) as nonincidental materials and supplies, or (2) in accordance with their accounting method. (See Chapter 10 for more on deducting inventory.)

Adding It All Up: The Value of Tax Deductions

Most taxpayers, even sophisticated businesspeople, don't fully appreciate just how much money they can save with tax deductions. Of course, only part of any deduction will end up back in your pocket as money saved. Because a deduction represents income on which you don't have to pay tax, the value of any deduction is the amount of tax you would have had to pay on that income had you not deducted it. So a deduction of $1,000 won't save you $1,000—it will save you whatever you would otherwise have had to pay as tax on that $1,000 of income.

Federal and State Income Taxes

To determine how much income tax a deduction will save you, you must first figure out your income tax bracket. The United States has a progressive income tax system for individual taxpayers. The higher your income, the higher your tax rate. As a result of the enactment of the Tax Cuts and Jobs Act, there are seven different tax rates (called tax brackets), ranging from 10% of taxable income to 37%. (See the chart below.)

You move from one bracket to the next only when your taxable income exceeds the bracket amount. For example, if you are a single taxpayer, you pay 10% income tax on all your taxable income up to $9,950 in 2021. If your taxable income exceeds that amount, the next tax rate (12%) applies to all your income over $9,950—but the 10% rate still applies to the first $9,950. If your income exceeds the 12% bracket amount, the next tax rate (22%) applies to the excess amount, and so on until the top bracket of 37% is reached.

The tax bracket in which the last dollar you earn for the year falls is called your marginal tax bracket. For example, if you have $85,000 in taxable income, your marginal tax bracket is 22%. To determine how much federal income tax a deduction will save you, multiply the amount of the deduction by your marginal tax bracket. For example, if your marginal tax bracket is 22%, you will save 22¢ in federal income taxes for every dollar you are able to claim as a deductible business expense (22% × $1 = 22¢).

The following table lists the 2021 federal income tax brackets for single and married individual taxpayers.

Income tax brackets are adjusted each year for inflation. For current brackets, see IRS Publication 505, *Tax Withholding and Estimated Tax*.

2021 Federal Personal Income Tax Brackets		
Rate	Married Filing Jointly	Individual Return
10%	$0–$19,900	$0–$9,950
12%	$19,901–$81,050	$9,951–$40,525
22%	$81,051–$172,750	$40,526–$86,375
24%	$172,751–$329,850	$86,376–$164,925
32%	$329,851–$418,850	$164,926–$209,425
35%	$418,851–$628,300	$209,426–$523,600
37%	Over $628,300	Over $523,600

You can also deduct your business expenses from any state income tax you must pay. The average state income tax rate is about 6%, although eight states (Alaska, Florida, Nevada, South Dakota, Tennessee, Texas, Washington, and Wyoming) don't have an income tax. (New Hampshire residents pay tax on gambling winnings and income earned through interest and dividends only.) You can find your state's tax rates at the Federation of Tax Administrators website at www.taxadmin.org.

State Income Tax Deductions May Differ
Generally, you may deduct the same business expenses for state tax purposes as you do for your federal taxes. However, some exceptions exist. You should contact your state tax agency for details. Every state tax agency has a website; you can find links to all of them at www.irs.gov/businesses/small-businesses-self-employed/state-government-websites.

Self-Employment Taxes

Everyone who works—business owner and employee alike—is required to pay Social Security and Medicare taxes. Employees pay one-half of these taxes through payroll deductions; the employer must pony up the other half and send the entire payment to the IRS. Business owners must pay all of these taxes themselves. Business owners' Social Security and Medicare contributions are called self-employment taxes.

Self-employment taxes consist of two separate taxes: the Social Security tax and the Medicare tax.

Social Security tax. The Social Security tax is a flat 12.4% tax on net self-employment income up to an annual ceiling that is adjusted for inflation each year. In 2021, the ceiling was $142,800 in net self-employment income. Thus, a person who had that much or more in income would pay $17,707 in Social Security taxes.

Medicare tax. There are two Medicare tax rates; a 2.9% tax is levied up to an annual ceiling—$200,000 for single taxpayers and $250,000 for married couples filing jointly. All income above that ceiling is taxed at a 3.8% rate. Thus, for example, a single taxpayer with $300,000 in net self-employment income would pay a 2.9% Medicare tax on the first $200,000 of income and a 3.8% tax on the remaining $100,000. This 0.9% Medicare tax increase applies to high-income employees as well as to the self-employed. Employees must pay a 2.35% Medicare tax